1980

NARRATION

FOUR LECTURES BY

GERTRUDE STEIN

WITH AN INTRODUCTION BY

THORNTON WILDER

GREENWOOD PRESS, PUBLISHERS
NEW YORK

INTRODUCTION

IN NOVEMBER of 1934 Miss Gertrude Stein delivered before an audience of five hundred students at the University of Chicago the lecture on "Poetry and Grammar" which is now printed in the volume entitled *Lectures in America*. At the invitation of the University she returned in March, 1935, to read before approximately the same audience the four lectures contained in this volume. In addition ten conferences were arranged during which Miss Stein amplified the ideas contained in these lectures by means of general discussion with some thirty selected students.

There are a number of ways in which these lectures may be approached. In the first place they are in themselves models of artistic form. The highly individual idiom in which they are written reposes upon an unerring ear for musical cadence and upon a conviction that repetition is a form of insistence and emphasis that is characteristic of all life, of history, and of nature itself. "If a thing is really existing there can be no repetition. . . . . Then we have insistence insistence that in its emphasis can never be repeating, because insistence is always alive and if it is alive it is never saying anything in the same way because emphasis can never be the same not even when it is most the same that is when it has been taught." In the printed version of the lectures the individuality of the idiom has been enhanced by the economy of the punctuation, which has been explained by Miss Stein as being a form of challenge to a livelier collaboration on the part of the reader. "A comma by helping you along holding your coat for you and putting on your shoes keeps you from living your life as actively as you should lead it. . . . . The longer, the more complicated the sentence the greater the number of the same kinds of words I had following one another, the more the very many more I had of them I felt the passionate need of their taking care of themselves by themselves and not helping them, and thereby enfeebling them by putting in a comma. . . . . A long complicated sentence should force itself upon you, make yourself know yourself knowing it."

Another approach to these lectures lies in seeing them as object-lessons of the teaching method. Nothing is learned save in answer to a deeply lodged and distinctly stated question. Beginning with a calculated simplicity, these lectures first prepare and provoke the correct questions in the listeners' minds. One is irresistibly reminded of the request that Dante put to his guide, and which might serve as a motto for all education:

> . . . io pregai che mi largisse il pasto
> Di cui largito m'aveva il disio.
> . . . I prayed him to bestow on me the food, for
> which he had already bestowed on me the appetite.

These are real rewards, but the great reward of these lectures lies in the richness and vitality of the ideas contained in them. We soon discover that we are not to hear about narration from the point of view that the rhetorics usually discuss the subject. We hear nothing of the proportion of exposition to narrative, of where to place a climax, of how to heighten vividness through the use of illustrative detail. Here we return to first principles, indeed: "Narration is what anybody has to say in any way about anything that can happen, that has happened or will happen in any way." There is an almost terrifying exactness in Miss Stein's use of the very words that the rest of the world employs so loosely: everybody, everything, and every way. Consequently the discussion leads at once into the realms of psychology, philosophy, and metaphysics, to a theory of knowledge and a theory of time. These matters are

vi

treated, however, not in the Latinizing jargon of the manuals, but in the homely language of colloquial usage. The great and exhilarating passage in the third lecture, describing the difference between "existing" and "happening," that begins: "The inside and the outside, the outside which is outside and the inside which is inside are not when they are inside and outside are not inside in short they are not existing, that is inside. . . . ."—such a passage might have been rendered in terms of "subjective and objective phenomena"; it might have been more academically impressive; it could not have been clearer; and it would have lost that quality of rising from the "daily life" and from our "common knowledge" which is the vitalizing character of Miss Stein's ideas.

These ideas are presented to us in a highly abstract form. Miss Stein pays her listeners the high compliment of dispensing for the most part with that apparatus of illustrative simile and anecdote that is so often employed to recommend ideas. She assumes that the attentive listener will bring, from a store of observation and reflection, the concrete illustration of her generalization. This is what renders doubly stimulating, for example, the treatment of the differences between English and American literature, and the distinction between prose and poetry—a critical principle which from the earlier lecture has already made so marked an impression and which in the present lectures receives a further development. In the present series, however, the outstanding passages will undoubtedly be those dealing with the psychology of the creative act as the moment of "recognition" and the discussion of the relations between the artist and the audience—a subject now the center of critical speculation in many quarters and which here receives distinguished and profound treatment.

Miss Stein has said that the artist is the most sensitive exponent of his contemporaneousness, expressing it while it still lies in the unconscious of society at large. In the first lecture in this book and in the lectures she has previously given she has described the character of the new points of view of this age, the twentieth century which was made by America, as the nineteenth was made by England, and with the result that "the United States is now the oldest country in the world." These lectures in their method and in their content are brilliant examples of the breadth and movement and energy that the perspective of time will reveal to have been our characteristic.

THORNTON WILDER

LECTURE 1

IT IS a rather curious thing that it should take a hundred years to change anything that is to change something, it is the human habit to think in centuries and centuries are more or less a hundred years and that makes a grandfather a grandmother to a grandson or a granddaughter if it happens right and it often does about happen right. Is it the human habit to think in centuries from a grandparent to a grandchild because it just does take about a hundred years for things to cease to have the same meaning that they had before, it is a curious thing a very curious thing that everything is a natural thing but it is it is a natural thing and it being a natural thing makes it a curious thing a very curious thing to almost anybody's feeling. One is always having to talk to one's self about it that a natural thing is not really a strange and a peculiar and a curious thing. So then there we are a hundred years does more or less make a century and this is determined by the fact that it includes a grandparent to a grandchild and that that is what makes it definitely different one time from another time and usually there is a war or a catastrophe to emphasize it so that any one can know it. It is a very strange thing that such a natural thing is inevitably to all of us such a strange thing such a striking thing such a disconcerting thing.

The eighteenth century finished with the French revolution and the Napoleonic wars the nineteenth century with the world war, but in each case the thing of course had been done the change had been made but the wars made everybody know it and liberated them from not knowing it not knowing that everything was not just exactly what it had been. I am quite sure that the world's history the world made up of human beings is made up in this way of

1

about always a century and it is determined that is made by the natural filling up of time from a grandparent to a grandchild. Twenty-five years roll around very quickly but four times twenty-five years which makes a century does not really roll around at all it makes a complete change but it does not roll around at all at least not to anybody's feeling.

That is what narrative is that twenty-five years roll around so quickly but that one hundred years do not roll around at all but that they end, the century ends in being an entirely different thing and so any century comes to begin and comes to end. That makes one of the great difficulties of narrative to begin and to end and I think it has to do with the fact that a century begins and ends but that no part of it begins and no part of it ends and this serious problem in narrative I will take up very much later but now first to know what English literature is in connection with English life and what American literature is in connection with their life and their lives because of course most literature is narrative that is in one way or in another way the telling of how anybody how everybody does anything and everything. To begin then with English literature and what it is and American literature and what it is.

But before going on to this matter I have just been thinking that the civil war in America was another case of about a century, seventeen sixty to eighteen sixty again made a grandfather to a granddaughter a grandmother to a grandson and so as usual everything changed as it always has done very likely it will do so again, very likely a century every so often will do what a century always has done.

But to commence again with what English literature has done in telling everything and what American literature has done in telling everything and how although they completely differ one from the other and they use the

2

same language to tell everything that can be happening it is naturally very naturally not at all the same thing.

I have already written a lot about what the English people are and what their literature is and how it changed in every century not how the English people changed the English people did not change. That is something that again we must remember as a contradiction that makes everything the same. Once a nation has lived long enough anywhere to be that nation and that commences very soon after they have come to live where they are to live the character of that nation can naturally never be changing. When they asked me when I came back to America do you find America changed I said no neither America nor Americans after all when you say changed how could they change what after all could they change to, and when you ask that of course there is no answer. How could there be any answer. After all how could they change what could they change to. Different things happen and at the end of more or less of a century the different things that have happened makes everybody do all the different things that have happened very differently, but they as a nation although they do do things differently do do those different things differently in the way they as that nation always has done them always will do them. And therefore any nation's literature is a homogeneous thing although in every century everything is different.

I do know about English literature that it has been determined by the fact that England is an island and that the daily life on that island was a completely daily life, that they could do nothing but lead a daily life on that island and that the more they owned everything outside of that island the more inevitably and completely were they forced to live the daily life in a more daily way, because if they owned everything outside they could not possibly allow

3

themselves to confuse the inside with the outside. Every hundred years or so everything changed, that they were English people living on an island did not change but things in relation one thing to another changed and that is what makes a century and in every century the relations of anything to anything changed and this change is what makes history, and really this is a thing for all of us to remember and to realize because it is going to make very clear the interesting thing that mostly history is not literature that literature is not history.

Literature we may say is what goes on all the time history is what goes on from time to time and this is what is terribly important to think about in connection with narrative.

But to come back again to English literature.

As I say the English people did different things the nations near them or around them did different things and about once every hundred years everybody became conscious of this thing that everybody had come to do different things that is to say had come to do the same things in a different way in a way so different that every one could come to know this thing know that it was a really different way and so of course a different way that had come to stay. That is inevitably what every one once every hundred or so years really comes to say. And this had happened in England in the same way as it happens anywhere where there is a grandfather or a grandmother to a grandson or a granddaughter. But all the time the English people were living their life every day, that had to be because that is what their island life had made them be that they lived their daily life every minute of the day. And the whole of English literature was a description of this daily life that they lived every day. And now there is another thing to say. If you live a daily life

4

every minute of the day the description of that daily life every day must be moving, it must fill you with complete emotion and it must at the same time be soothing. It must be completing as emotion and it must be soothing. If you live your daily life every minute of the whole day there must really be very little excitement in the narrative with which you while the time away that is natural enough if you think about it and a great deal of the written narrative in English literature has to do with this thing, they want narrative they need narrative because as they live their daily life every minute of the day narrative has so much to say it has to say that that daily life is being lived every second of that day. And that is what literature does it emphasizes what every one has as the life of the nation which the life of every one in that nation makes it be. That is what literature is as anybody can see if they read the writing as a nation makes it be.

It makes it be absolutely clear that the daily life in England is a daily life lived every minute of the day. That is to say. The minutes succeeding each other each one has in it in the daily living that minutes succeed each other give them and every one knowing that daily living is going on in each one of them can know this in them in each minute of them and each minute can give any one this thing, that daily living is existing.

Americans and English use the same language but the Americans have not a daily living as any Englishman does and can have.

In America life goes on but not from minute to minute and each minute being filled full with it.

Therefore Americans do not need a narrative of every day of any day, they have nothing to tell of the living of every moment in a daily living, they have nothing to say of living every day that makes it be a really soothing thing to say. Think of any American narrative and what it has to say.

Not at all.

One may say that in America there is no daily life at all.

The English live their island life every day every minute of the day and if there could be one moment in the day in which their daily life was not lived in the daily island way their narrative would be at an end there would be nothing to say. Now the English write their narrative in English because that is the language they have made and it is made to tell of a daily life lived every minute of the day. Also as it is a daily life lived every minute of the day it is a soothing thing to say and mostly what the English have had to say has been that it has been a soothing thing to say that they live every minute of the day even when the day has been a difficult day.

Now the Americans also tell their story in English, but as they have no daily life every minute of every day and as the language is written down so much any and every day they can not change that language and still they have nothing to say no narrative to tell about living every day no narrative to soothe any one who is living every minute of every day.

So what can they do.

At any other time at a time when everybody and everything is not being written all the time it would have been an easy thing to make the language the Americans are using another language but now it is almost impossible to do this. Little by little it does not change the words they use continue to be all the same and yet the narrative they have to tell has nothing whatever to do with the narrative the English have and had to tell.

The American not living every minute of every day in a daily way does not make what he has to say to be soothing he wants what he has to say to be exciting, and to move as everything moves, not to move as emotion is moving but to move as anything that really moves is moving.

6

It is going to be very interesting and it is very interesting and it has been very interesting to see how two nations having the same words all the same grammatical construction have come to be telling things that have nothing whatever in common.

It is something that any one interested in narrative has to very much think about, because it has never happened before. Always before the language of each nation who had a narrative to make a story to tell a life to express a thing to say did it with a language that had gradually become a language that was made gradually by them to say what they had to say. But here in America because the language was made so late in the day that is at a time when everybody began to read and to write all the time and to read what was written all the time it was impossible that the language would be made as languages used to be made to say what the nation which was coming to be was going to say. All this has never happened before. History repeats itself anything repeats itself but all this had never happened before.

So what has there been and what is there and what is there going to be to do about it. That narrative is going to be made that the story they have to tell is going to be told that the nation which lives in a land that has made it that nation will have to tell its story in its own way about that there can be no doubt, the story must be told will be told can be told but they will tell this story they tell this story using the exactly same words that were made to tell an entirely different story and the way it is being done the pressure being put upon the same words to make them move in an entirely different way is most exciting, it excites the words it excites us who use them. These words that were made by those who finally made them to tell the story of the soothing of living every minute of the day a daily living these words by the pressure

7

of being used by those who never any day live a daily living have not come to have a different meaning not at all but they have come to have a different movement in them and this is all so very very exciting and interesting and unexpectedly a real thing. As always it has taken a century for anybody to really completely know this thing about the language we use we Americans use to tell that there is in us for us by us and with us no daily daily living.

So then we must really realize that the language the English language was made by the English people to tell this thing that the daily living the daily island living is every moment existing and that any and every Englishman is always conscious of the necessary existing every minute of his living of the daily living which makes him an Englishman with a daily island living, this is true of Englishmen Englishwomen and English children.

There is never a moment in the day when the English people do not live their daily living every day their daily island living every day, and this as the language formed itself to tell what the people who made it had to tell of how they lived every day they lived in their daily way every moment of the day it changed from the language as it began in Chaucer's day to the nineteenth century when it completely told in every way that they lived their daily life every moment of every day.

Think well of English literature and you will see what I mean.

As I said in the nineteenth century as the sun never set upon the English flag and that island owned everything outside they had more and more to tell every minute of every day that they were leading their daily living every moment of every day because otherwise the outside might come to be inside and the inside might come to be outside and then their way of telling about the way they lived their daily living every day would have gone away.

And so by the time the English language had its final form made by the English who had made a language it was a language that could completely soothingly movingly say that they lived their daily life every day.

So there they were and the Americans were not at all that way they did not live their life at all no not at all in that way and they had it to say that they lived their own life in their own way and they had it to say it with the words that had been made to tell a nation's story in an entirely different way as the nation who had made the language had the entirely different story to tell of living their daily life every moment of every day.

You do understand if you think about it that the American people do not live their daily life in every minute of every day.

Think about it and you will see that you do realize that. Think about how the American lives his life and you must realize that although he is alive any day unless he is dead never the less he does not in any way feel himself as living his daily life every moment of any day.

And so we have this situation, a settled language because a language is settled after it does not change any more that is as to words and grammar, and it being written so completely written all the time it inevitably cannot change much and yet the pressure upon these words to make them do something that they did not do for those who made that language come to exist is a very interesting thing to watch.

If you watch as I have watched all through the history of American literature you will see how the pressure of the non daily life living of the American nation has forced the words to have a different feeling of moving. I like to look at it in its last expression in the road signs which are a further concentration of the thing they did to the words in advertising. They got the words to express moving and in England the words even when they were most active were words that expressed arrested motion or a very slow succession. In the American writing the words began to have inside themselves those same words that in the English were completely quiet or very slowly moving began to have within themselves the consciousness of completely moving, they began to detach themselves from the solidity of anything, they began to excitedly feel themselves as if they were anywhere or anything, think about American writing from Emerson, Hawthorne Walt Whitman Mark Twain Henry James myself Sherwood Anderson Thornton Wilder and Dashiell Hammitt and you will see what I mean, as well as in advertising and in road signs, you will see what I mean, words left alone more and more feel that they are moving and all of it is detached and is detaching anything from anything and in this detaching and in this moving it is being in its way creating its existing. This is then the real difference between English and American writing and this then can then lead to anything.

I can say it enough but can I say it more than enough that the daily life is a daily life if at any moment of the daily life that daily life is all there is of life.

Can I say it more than often enough.

Can I say more than often enough that the daily life if it is not a daily life consists in at no moment of that daily living of there being any conscious feeling or unconscious feeling that at every moment of that daily living daily living is all there is of any living.

In America they may have daily occupations they do not have to they may but they do not have to they often do not they often do but whether they do or whether they do not do so do not have the daily occupation in any case

10

that daily occupation does not force upon them any necessity of having every and any moment of their daily life that they are living their daily living.

Think of the American life as it is lived, they all move so much even when they stay still and they do very often stay still they all move so much. They move so much because in moving they know for certain they can know it any way but in moving they really know it really know it as certain that they are not daily living in their daily living. The English just in the other way even when they are travelling are not moving, they do not move no one can move who is really living in any moment of their living their daily living.

And this is the thing that is a necessary thing to have in exchange of anything of words or what any one is doing.

In the early English writing words did move around they moved by themselves we get that with the period that ended with the end of the Elizabethans, words moved then, they made their own existing they were there and they enjoyed that thing they enjoyed being there the words did and any one having anything to do with them anything to do with the words being there knew that of them knew that the words were enjoying that thing were enjoying being there.

That made the period that we call Elizabethan, that was really the end of words living by being existing. Then slowly as I say words began to have another meaning, they were used to accept everything as being there in the daily living they accepted their being there to tell something or to make everything have emotion have sentimental feeling or to be soothing. That is what makes daily life when it is lived at any moment of the day or night, that anything should be there and it should be there and should be there to be soothing and it should be there to give existence the emotion of sentimental

11

feeling, the emotion of anything and of everything being there as anything and everything is.

Now it has often been said that the Americans in their feeling about the English language they are using have some connection with the Elizabethan way of using the English they are using.

This is not really true. The early English through the Elizabethans used words in every way they like the lively way the words had the words that would later be there to stay but now had come there and coming there had all the excitement of arriving in any way they could arrive and they were arriving in every kind of a way.

That made them use the language the English language in their way and it is and was a wonderful way but it is not at all the way we are using the language that has really come to stay. Because there is no doubt about it that English language that we all use has come to stay, we are changing grammar and punctuation and shoving it around and putting pressure upon it but there it is and it has certainly as any American is bound to say it has come as it is it has come to stay.

Now wherein is our use of it so different and it is completely different from the way the English used it in the early day when it was first coming if not coming to stay and then later when the nineteenth century had it as a language that had completely and entirely come to do nothing really do nothing but stay.

It has been said that our use of the English language has some connection with the Elizabethans and that has been said because at that time the English language moved around, words were themselves and having been discovered and having been exciting by being next to each other were gaily and happily alive and every one who had anything to do with them felt that way about them. The words themselves at that time did not decide what they were to do in the way that the meaning should come out of them but every one who did anything with them was excited by the way any one could use any one of them and how wonderful it was to do what any one was doing with them. That made the liveliness of the period ending with the Elizabethans that every one liked everything that any word was and liked anything that any one could do with any one of them any word or all the words that were there then, but and that is where it was very different from the American way of using those words they did not want the words the settled words the known words to act in a particularly that is to move in a particular way and also in any kind of a direction.

The English from Chaucer to the Elizabethans played with words they endlessly played with words because it was such an exciting thing to have them there words that had come to be the words they had just come to use then.

But the American has a different feeling, these words the words that the Englishman had settled into having as a steady and unchangeable something, they the Americans did not care for the particular use these later Englishmen had come to have for them and the American had then decided that any word which was a word which was there if you put enough pressure upon them if you arranged and concentrated and took away all excrescences from them you could make these same words do what you needed to do with them.

And they did this thing and they are doing this thing and punctuation and arranging them and destroying any connection between them between the words that would that did when the English used them make of them having a beginning and a middle and an ending to them has made of these English words words that move as the Americans move with them move always move and in every and in any direction. It is a very interesting thing that this this has been done a very interesting thing that this has been done by the pressure brought to bear upon them brought to bear upon these words which came to us as they were and as they still are but now they have an entirely different movement in them.

Anybody can tell this the minute they pick up any ordinary book any ordinary newspaper any ordinary advertisement or read any ordinary road sign or slang or conversation. The words used are the same words but they have such a different pressure put upon them that in the case of the English the words have the feeling of containing that in which they are staying and with the American they have the feeling that they are and indicate and feel moving existing inside in them.

And so there is all this and twenty-five years move around so quickly and a century does not move around at all and at any time that is to say at some time a century will have its ending and its beginning and after all why not after all since after all after all nothing so any American can know nothing does need to have a middle and ending and a beginning and certainly at the end of every century or so at the end of a grandfather to a granddaughter at the end of a grandmother to a grandson, there will be that every one has something that is no longer anything and still if you have had always had had a daily life in every moment of your living that is not changing and your language will have the words feeling that thing feeling that they are there and staying and if you have not any day your daily living as an American

14

never can have and never does have any day in his living then the words which are their words will have in them the feeling of moving even if by spelling and lettering they are the same words that the English have who have in them the feeling of staying.

And so this is what I have to say about our language which is our language today and in our way as any words are are our words to-day.

I like the feeling of words doing as they want to do and as they have to do when they live where they have to live that is where they have come to live which of course they do do.

LECTURE 2

I HAVE said and anybody can say anybody might say that knowledge is what you know. Knowledge is what you know and there is nothing more difficult to say than that that knowledge is what you know.

Let's make our flour meal and meat in Georgia.

Is that prose or poetry and why.

Let's make our flour meal and meat in Georgia.

This is a sign I read as we rode on a train from Atlanta to Birmingham and I wondered then and am still wondering is it poetry or is it prose let's make our flour meal and meat in Georgia, it might be poetry and it might be prose and of course there is a reason why a reason why it might be poetry and a reason why it might be prose.

Does let's make our flour meal and meat in Georgia move in various ways and very well and has that to do really to do with narrative in poetry, has it really to do with narrative at all and is it more important in poetry that a thing should move in various kinds of ways than it is in prose supposing both of them to be narrative. I think about these things a great deal these days because things anything any one can see does move move about and just move in various kinds of ways and sometimes I wonder if that makes poetry and sometimes I wonder if that makes prose and now I wonder is there any such thing as poetry is there any such thing as prose or is it just that now anything moves about in various ways it sometimes stays still but a great deal it does move about in various ways. Since what you know is what you know do you or do you not know this.

16

There are now several questions is there anything that is not narrative and what is narrative what has narrative gotten to be now. When one used to think of narrative one meant a telling of what is happening in successive moments of its happening the quality of telling depending upon the conviction of the one telling that there was a distinct succession in happening, that one thing happened after something else and since that happening in succession was a profound conviction in every one then really there was no difference whether any one began in the beginning or the middle or the ending because since narrative was a progressive telling of things that were progressively happening it really did not make any difference where you were at what moment you were in your happening since the important part of telling anything was the conviction that anything that everything was progressively happening. But now we have changed all that we really have. We really now do not really know that anything is progressively happening and as knowledge is what you know and as now we do not know that anything is progressively happening where are we then in narrative writing and what has this to do with poetry and with prose if it has that is to say if poetry and prose have anything to do with anything and anything has anything to do with narrative that is the telling of what is happening.

I know what poetry and prose has been and I have been telling this thing telling what poetry and prose has been and when I told it I said it in this way. This is what I said about what poetry and prose has been.

Does telling anything as it is being needed being telling now by any one does it mean cutting loose from anything, no because there is nothing to cut loose from. Remember this that is do not remember but know this when there is no more to tell about what prose and poetry has been.

It is funny that Americans that an American who has always believed that they were the people knowing everything about repression are really the ones who have naturally been moving in the direction that there is nothing to cut loose from.

So to begin to tell what I did tell because I knew it then very very well what prose and poetry has been.

I said prose concerned itself with the internal balance of sentences which are things that exist in and for themselves and are not complete as anything because anything existing in and for itself does not have to have completion, if it exists in and for itself there is no relation of it to it and therefore there is no element of completion, it is a thing that exists by internal balancing that is what a sentence is and since that is what a sentence is or rather what a sentence was perhaps now there is no longer any need for a sentence to be existing perhaps not, in any case certainly that is what a sentence has been a thing that by internal balancing made itself what it was. I further have said and do say that a succession of these sentences were used in paragraphing and that these sentences existing in that way and being included by a paragraphing ending made not by their balancing but by the need of progression made a paragraph that had an emotional meaning while the sentence itself had none. This is what I said the sentence and the paragraph had been has been and now let me say it again.

Let me say again what the sentence and the paragraph has been and what has been its relation to narrative that is the telling of anything.

Narrative has been the telling of anything because there has been always has been a feeling that something followed another thing that there was succession in happening.

18

In a kind of a way what has made the Old Testament such permanently good reading is that really in a way in the Old Testament writing there really was not any such thing there was not really any succession of anything and really in the Old Testament there is really no sentence existing and no paragraphing, think about this thing, think if you have not really been knowing this thing and then let us go on telling about what paragraphs and sentences have been what prose and poetry has been. So then in the Old Testament writing there is really no actual conclusion that anything is progressing that one thing is succeeding another thing, that anything in that sense in the sense of succeeding happening is a narrative of anything, but most writing is based on this thing most writing has been a real narrative writing a telling of the story of anything in the way that thing has been happening and now everything is not that thing there is at present not a sense of anything being successively happening, moving is in every direction beginning and ending is not really exciting, anything is anything, anything is happening and anybody can know anything at any time that anything is happening and so really and truly is there any sentence and any paragraphing is there prose and poetry as the same thing or different things is there now any narrative of any successive thing.

I always remember during the war being so interested in one thing in seeing the American soldiers standing, standing and doing nothing standing for a long time not even talking but just standing and being watched by the whole French population and their feeling the feeling of the whole population that the American soldier standing there and doing nothing impressed them as the American soldier as no soldier could impress by doing anything. It is a much more impressive thing to any one to see any one standing, that is not in action than acting or doing anything doing anything being a successive thing, standing not being a successive thing but being something existing. That is then the difference between narrative as it has been and narrative as it is now. And this has come to be a natural thing in a perfectly natural way that the narrative of to-day is not a narrative of succession as all the writing for a good many hundreds of years has been.

And so to begin again with what I have said that poetry and prose has been that sentences and paragraphs have been that narrative has been.

I said then that sentences as they have for centuries been written were a balancing a complete inner balance of something that stated something as being existing and that a paragraph was a succession of these sentences that going on and then stopping made the emotional content of something having a beginning and middle and ending. Sentences are contained within themselves and anything really contained within itself has no beginning or middle or ending, any one can know this thing by knowing anything at any moment of their living, in short by knowing anything. How do you know anything, well you know anything as complete knowledge as having it completely in you at the actual moment that you have it. That is what knowledge is, and essentially therefore knowledge is not succession but an immediate existing. All these things then are as they are and we come back to what poetry is what prose is and the reason why and what it all has to do with narrative and whether any narrative is existing now and how and why.

Knowledge then is what you know at the time at any time that you really know anything. And in knowing anything you know it as you know it, you know it at the time that you are knowing it and in that way the way of knowing it knowing has not succession there may be continuous states of knowing anything but at no time of knowing is there anything but knowing that thing the thing you know, know carefully what you do know and of course anybody can know that this is so. And once more I say the Old Testament is the thing that has the way of knowing anything as knowing anything and not feeling or thinking about anything succeeding anything. Knowing is knowing anything at the knowing the thing when that thing is what you know. The Old Testament has always been so. So there we are and in a curious way we now and in this day at this time have come again to have this as our own, that there is no succession, there is moving in any and any various direction and that being a thing existing knowing is what you know at the moment anything is being as knowing. The exciting thing about all this is that as it is new it is old and as it is old it is new, but now really we have come to be in our way which is an entirely different way from the way the Old Testament had its way we have come to be that knowledge is what you know when you know and as you know there is no succession of what you know since you do know what you know. Any one really any one can really know that this is so.

To come back again to what prose was and what poetry was and what it is if it is going to be prose and poetry again. Perhaps it is not going to be prose and poetry again. Nothing really changes everything is as it was but perhaps it is not going to be prose and poetry again perhaps it is not poetry and prose now in spite of anything and everything being always having been what it was.

So to begin again about what prose and poetry has been.

Prose has been a thing made of sentences and paragraphs, the sentences saying a thing and then one after the other the sentences making a paragraph the thing by reason of it succeeding one sentence succeeding another one come finally to giving a beginning and ending and a middle to anything in other words having it that a paragraph has come to give a thing the emotion that anything having a beginning and a middle and an ending can give to anything. Think of narrative from this thing, a narrative can give emotion because an emotion is dependent upon succession upon a thing having a beginning and a middle and an ending. That is why every one used to like sequels and some still do anybody still may but actually in modern writing sequels have no meaning do you begin to see now why I say that sentences and paragraphs need not necessarily go on existing. Do you begin to see what I mean by saying this thing.

So then prose has been for a long time has been made of sentences and paragraphs, sentences which within themselves carry no emotion because a thing balanced within itself does not give out nor have within any emotion but sentences existing within themselves by the balance that holds them when they are in succession one after the other and make a paragraph have the emotion that any succession can give to anything. A sentence has not really any beginning or middle or ending because each part is its part as its part and so the whole exists within by the balance within but the paragraph exists not by a balance within but by a succession. Anybody really anybody can realize this thing and realizing this thing can realize that narrative up to the present time has been not a succession of paragraphing but a continuing of paragraphing, a quite entirely different thing.

Let me explain again.

A sentence is inside itself by its internal balancing, think how a sentence is made by its parts of speech and you will see that it is not dependent upon a

22

beginning a middle and an ending but by each part needing its own place to make its own balancing, and because of this in a sentence there is no emotion, a sentence does not give off emotion. But one sentence coming after another sentence makes a succession and the succession if it has a beginning a middle and an ending as a paragraph has does form create and limit an emotion.

So now we really do know what sentences and paragraphs are and they have to do everything in narrative writing the way narrative has been written. Because as narrative has mostly been written it is dependent upon things succeeding upon a thing having a beginning and a middle and an ending.

Now these are two things do not forget that they are not one thing. Succeeding one thing succeeding another thing is succeeding and having a beginning a middle and an ending is entirely another thing.

When I first began writing really just began writing, I was tremendously impressed by anything by everything having a beginning a middle and an ending. I think one naturally is impressed by anything having a beginning a middle and an ending when one is beginning writing and that is a natural thing because when one is emerging from adolescence, which is really when one first begins writing one feels that one would not have been one emerging from adolescence if there had not been a beginning and a middle and an ending to anything. So paragraphing is a thing then any one is enjoying and sentences are less fascinating, but then gradually well if you are an American gradually you find that really it is not necessary not really necessary that anything that everything has a beginning and a middle and an ending and so you struggling with anything as anything has begun and begun and began does not really mean that thing does not really mean beginning or begun.

I found myself at this time quite naturally using the present participle, in The Making of Americans I could not free myself from the present participle because dimly I felt that I had to know what I knew and I knew that the beginning and middle and ending was not where I began.

So then that was the way prose was written and that was narrative writing as I say practically with everything the average English reading person was reading or writing with the exception of the Old Testament yes with the exception of the Old Testament which was not English writing, it was the writing of another kind of living, it was the writing whose beginning and middle and ending was really not existing was a writing where events in succession were not existing, where events one succeeding another event was not at all exciting no not at all exciting.

So now we know how narrative prose was and is written and now let us begin to think about how poetry was written and had that too any sense of succession of one thing succeeding another thing as the thing really producing emotion really holding the attention.

Yes I must have you have to hold it as I have to have you have it that gradually as English literature came more and more to be written it came always more and more to have it that it needed to have emotion in it the emotion that only could come from everything having something that came before and after that thing. In the earlier poetry in English writing it was there of course it was always there but they could feel something without feeling that thing that anything could only be anything if it was succeeding some other thing, and finally then English writing was entirely that thing, in its poetry as well as in its narrative writing that one thing came after another thing and that not anything existing aroused any one to feeling but

24

that a thing having beginning and middle and ending made every one have the emotion they had about anything. Did this make poetry as well as prose then. Yes it did.

The fact that anything was existing was moving around by itself in any way it wanted to move did not arouse any emotion it was only anything succeeding any other thing anything having middle and beginning and ending could and did and would arouse emotion.

A great deal perhaps all of my writing of The Making of Americans was an effort to escape from this thing to escape from inevitably feeling that anything that everything had meaning as beginning and middle and ending.

And it was right and quite a natural thing that the book I wrote in which I was escaping from the inevitable narrative of anything of everything succeeding something of needing to be succeeding that is following anything of anything of everything consisting that is the emotional and the actual value of anything counting in anything having beginning and middle and ending it was natural that the book I wrote in which I was escaping from all this inevitably in narrative writing I should have called The Making of Americans. I did not call it this for that reason but I called it this and this is what is happening, American writing has been an escaping not an escaping but an existing without the necessary feeling of one thing succeeding another thing of anything having a beginning and a middle and an ending.

And now all this has everything to do with poetry and prose and whether now whether there really is now any such thing.

Poetry and prose. I came to the conclusion that poetry was a calling an intensive calling upon the name of anything and that prose was not the using the name of anything as a thing in itself but the creating of sentences that

were self-existing and following one after the other made of anything a continuous thing which is paragraphing and so a narrative that is a narrative of anything. That is what a narrative is of course one thing following any other thing.

If poetry is the calling upon a name until that name comes to be anything if one goes on calling on that name more and more calling upon that name as poetry does then poetry does make of that calling upon a name a narrative it is a narrative of calling upon that name. That is what poetry has been and as it has been that thing as it has been a calling upon a name instead of a succession of internal balancing as prose has been then naturally at the time all the time the long time after the Elizabethans poetry and prose has not been the same thing no not been at all the same thing. Before the end of the Elizabethans and then in the eighteenth century when the inner balancing of sentences really invaded poetry and poetry was less the calling upon a name of anything than it was an inner balancing of anything, Pope is an excellent example it is hard telling really about the eighteenth century whether there is any really any internal feeling that makes poetry poetry and a different thing from prose.

But during the nineteenth century there was no doubt no doubt about it. Prose was the sentence and paragraphing and the use not of nouns but of parts of speech that made their use that use and poetry was the calling upon names the really calling upon names. There has always been this real difference between prose and poetry, that prose is dependent upon the sentence and then upon the paragraph and poetry upon the calling upon names. There have been some centuries never forget that a century is always more or less about one hundred years, but always there has been this difference

26

and now well now is there this difference is there this difference and if not why not.

Very well then.

It is certain that there has been this thing prose and poetry and narrative which is roughly a telling of anything where anything happens after any other thing.

In the beginning there really was no difference between poetry and prose in the beginning of writing in the beginning of talking in the beginning of hearing anything or about anything. How could there be how could there have been since the name of anything was then as important as anything as anything that could be said about anything. Once more I tell you that the Old Testament did this thing there was not really any difference between prose and poetry then, they told what they were and they felt what they saw and they knew how they knew and everything they had to say came as it had to come to do what it had to do.

Really can you say that there was any difference between prose and poetry then. No not at all. Not then.

And then slowly they came to know that what they knew might mean something different from what they had known it was when they knew simply knew what it was. And so they began telling about it then how one thing meant something then and how something else meant something else then and in poetry they tried to say what they knew as they knew it and then more and more then they simply tried to name it and that made poetry then, anything made poetry then and they told anything and as they told anything they felt it as a telling of anything and so it meant more and more that they called it by its name as they knew it and that more and more made poetry then.

27

At the same time as I say they began to feel what they said when they said anything when they knew anything and this made them then think about how they said anything how they knew anything and in telling this thing telling how they knew anything how they said anything prose began, and so then there was prose and poetry. Before that there had been only one thing, the one thing any one knew as they knew anything.

Prose and poetry then went on and more and more as it went on prose was more and more telling and by sentences balancing and then by paragraphing prose was more and more telling how anything happened if any one had anything to say about what happened how anything was known if any one had anything to say about how anything was known, and poetry poetry tried to remain with knowing anything and knowing its name, gradually it came to really not knowing but really only knowing its name and that is at last what poetry became.

And now.

Well and now, now that we have been realizing that anything having a beginning and middle and ending is not what is making anything anything, and now that everything is so completely moving the name of anything is not really anything to interest any one about anything, now it is coming that once again nobody can be certain that narrative is existing that poetry and prose have different meanings.

Let's make our flour meal and meat in Georgia.

Well believe it or not it is very difficult to know whether that is prose or poetry and does it really make any difference if you do or do not know. This.

And so things moving perhaps perhaps moving in any direction, names being not existing because anybody can know what any body else is talking about without any name being mentioning, without any belief in any name being existing, I have just been trying to write the history of some one if his name had not been the name he had and I have called it Four In America and it is very interesting. You can slowly change any one by their name changing to any other name, and so slowly just knowing the name of anything and so making any one remember about such a thing the thing whose name its name anybody has happened to be mentioning cannot really very much interest any one, not really very much, and so perhaps narrative and poetry and prose have all come where they do not have to be considered as being there. Perhaps not I very much really very much think perhaps not, and that may make one thing or anything or everything say itself in a different way yes in a different way, who shall say, and all this now and always later we will come to say, perhaps yes, perhaps no, no and yes are still nice words, yes I guess I still will believe that I will.

You will perhaps say no and yes perhaps yes.

LECTURE 3

NARRATIVE concerns itself with what is happening all the time, history concerns itself with what happens from time to time. And that is perhaps what is the matter with history and that is what is perhaps the matter with narrative.

I am now going to talk not about the successes in narrative and history but the way they who write narrative and history do not do what they say they will do when they start out to do what they are about to do.

Let us think of newspapers, of novels, of detective stories of biographies of autobiographies of histories and of conversations. Let us think about them. I do not say let us know about them because it is hard to know what you do know about a thing that does not do what it does do.

And so what does the newspaper do and what does it not do.

But before we begin with anything that does or does not do what it is to do what it says it would if it could do that thing let us think again of narrating anything of beginning anything of ending anything.

It does happen it is bound to happen that the way of telling anything can come not to mean anything to the one telling that thing. When that does happen that the way of telling anything has come not to mean anything to the one telling that thing perhaps then one does go on telling the thing in the way that telling that thing does not mean that thing to the one telling that thing or one stops telling anything or one starts telling that thing in some other way that may or may not come to mean anything.

The choice of one of these three things is of course a perfectly natural thing although it is usually called experimenting because it is really not experi-

30

menting, experimenting is trying to do some thing in a way that may produce a result which is a desired result by the person doing it but telling something is not an experiment it is a thing that has to be done since any one since every one inevitably has to tell something and has to tell something in the way that makes it feel that that something is what that thing is.

That is what narrative is and always at a time no one can go on telling anything in the way he has been telling that thing because no one is listening and even if that does not make any difference to him then he himself is not listening and perhaps eventually that does that can that will that may make a difference to him. Anything may make a difference to any one but that certainly can or may make a difference all the difference any of the difference to him.

Think about how any one is no longer listening when some one is telling something and you will know all about this thing.

Narrative is what anybody has to say in any way about anything that can happen has happened will happen in any way.

That is what narrative is and so of course there always is narrative and anybody can stop listening to any way of telling anything. This undoubtedly can and does happen, even if it is exciting enough or has been. Anybody can stop listening to any telling of anything.

And this brings us to everything how anything is told will be told or has been.

There we are.

What do you tell and how do you tell it.

If you tell it very well how do you tell it and if you do not tell it very well if you do not tell it well at all how do you tell it.

This anybody knows since everybody is everybody and everybody is always one or many of them to always tell it.

There are many ways that anybody has that is anybody who is everybody and everybody and anybody is anybody and everybody there are many ways that they have to tell what they tell and to have anybody or themselves or everybody or not themselves or any combination of themselves or any combination of anybody or everybody to listen to it, listen while they tell it.

This makes narrative and at any time there is a great deal of it anybody can say at any time that there is not enough or just enough or too much of it. Anyway anybody everybody can say anything about narrative their own or anybody else's narrative but one thing is certain and sure that anybody telling everything even if it is nothing that they are telling or is either telling what they want to tell what they have to tell what they like to tell or what they will tell they tell a narrative.

Sometime anybody can get tired of it and when everybody who is anybody does get tired of it then that is the end the natural end of that way of telling it.

That is what happens what has happened when everybody begins to think in a kind of a way which is a different way and that can happen of course it can. Feelings may have something to do with it or they may not have anything to do with it. Let it alone if you like let anything alone if you like but feelings are feelings and they are always there but anybody can have any way of telling anything they are telling about it. That makes a narrative and does a narrative have to have a beginning and an ending.

To know about this you have to look at country to see what it looks like, since land and water looks not like itself but is the whole of it, and therefore is there any beginning and ending to it. Is there, are there not two things

32

to think about it are there not, about beginning and ending but later very much later we will go into that but now to consider the perfectly ordinary ways narrative has been written, newspapers, novels, detective stories, biography autobiography history conversations, letter-writing whatever kind of way any of these things are written makes no difference a narrative is any kind of way of trying to tell anything any one has to tell about anything that is or was or will be happening, and any kind of telling is the telling of what is happening inside or outside but is the telling the natural the immediate the necessary telling of anything that is happening. Now the newspapers have been and are very interesting as being one way one variation of one way in it if you like but one way of telling anything of telling everything of telling something.

What do the newspapers do and how do they do it, and what is the matter with it that is if there is anything the matter with it.

But to go back again just a little again to the way anybody or everybody tells anything anything about anything that is happening all the various ways there is of doing it and all the different ways anybody that is everybody can or cannot get tired of listening to it.

Think about it anybody listens to it as you yourself tell anything and as you yourself or any one listen while you yourself or any one tell anything. It is extraordinary how few and how many ways there are of telling anything listen to yourself and you will know something of all about it and how few and yet how extraordinarily varied ways there are of listening or of getting tired of listening to it.

All this makes anything written interesting to any one interested in it the number of ways any one tells anything theatre novels history poetry biography

33

autobiography newspapers letter-writing and conversations and the number of ways anybody that is everybody gets tired of listening to it. Everybody always has to be listening to something, that is the way it is always anybody has to be listening to something that is what makes life lived the way that is what makes anybody who they are what they are, of course it does any of you think of your life the way it is, you are always listening to some one to something and you are always telling something to some one or to any one. That is life the way it is lived.

I once said and I think it is true that being a genius is being one who is one at one and at the same time telling and listening to anything or everything.

Any of you try it and you will see what a difficult thing it is to listen to anything and everything in the way any one is telling anything and at the same time while you are listening to be telling inside yourself and outside yourself anything that is happening everything that is anything. That is what genius is to be always going on doing this thing at one and at the same time listening and telling really listening and really telling.

That is the reason why so often people have genius when they are twenty one, talent when they are thirty one, repetition of this talent when they are forty one and then nothing of anything that can make any one listen to any of them after forty one. This is of course a well known thing but if you notice any and every one you will see how naturally this thing does happen. When you are young you have an energy that makes hearing and telling beginning over all at one time, but you grow older and when you listen you can not be telling anything and when you tell anything you cannot hear anything and so then what was begun when you are young and had energy often for two things does not go on.

34

This is a sad story and does happen so often that there is no use continuing to sadden any one by going on.

I do not cannot believe that anything is or can be more interesting than the way and the fact that everybody is always telling everything and that anybody can in their way go on listening or not go on listening. But everybody can feel about telling and about listening like that. Anybody can.

So now about the newspapers what are they telling how are they telling what do they intend to tell about what they tell and who listens who does listen. It is very interesting.

Newspapers want to do something, they want to tell what is happening as if it were just then happening. They want to write that happening as if it was happening on the day the newspapers are read that is not as if the thing was happening on the day the newspaper is read a little that all the same but as if the writing were being written as it is read, that is what they mean by hot off the press, but yet after all there is an interval generally six hours or so but always an interval, and that interval they try to bridge by head lines, and do they succeed, not very well I guess not very well because it is not possible to tell in the way they have to tell a thing that is told as a reality, all this has an awful lot to do with the writing of history.

As I say what does the newspaper really want to do and what does anybody who reads the newspaper want to feel that they want the newspaper to do.

Really what the newspaper does really want to do and what the reader of the newspaper wants the newspaper to do is to know every day what happened the day before and so get the feeling that it has happened on the same day the day the newspaper appeared the day the newspaper reader reads the

35

newspaper and not on the day before. If they did not want to do and to have this thing the newspaper reader and the newspaper writer then they would not mind so much reading the newspaper of the day before and anybody knows that anybody who reads newspapers always objects to reading the newspaper of the day before.

Well there are two things about it, the newspaper reader wants to read the newspaper every day because he wants the idea of happenings happening every day and if there is a day without the happening of that day which is really the happening of the day before then the newspaper reader feels that it is like the sun standing still or any abnormal thing there is a day and nothing has happened on that day.

That makes anybody feel that you cannot call a day a day if it is not a day if nothing that had been happening has happened on that day.

That is really what the newspaper has to say that everything that has happened has happened on that day but really this is not true because everything that has happened on that day on the newspaper day has really happened the day before and that makes all the trouble that there is with the newspaper as it is and in every way they try to destroy this day the day between the day before and the day the newspaper day. Of course by day I naturally mean night too but the newspaper really does not know and so it cannot really say that there is really any difference between the night and the day. That is another of the difficulties they have in face of the real trouble that the newspaper day is always the day before the newspaper day and yet that is what they really have to say that the newspaper day is the day it is, which of course it is not.

And so everything in the newspaper begins with its not being so and that like everything complicates and makes difficult telling and listening, it may

36

complicate and the newspaper does by making it too easy, so much do they have to deceive the reader into feeling that yesterday is to-day that they have to make it too easy and in making it too easy they do do something they had not intended to do they make it no longer an exciting thing to do because they have commenced to do too well what if they did have it to do it would be impossible to do.

Do you see what I mean.

It is very interesting.

And it has an awful lot to do with everything.

There are so many things to say at one time and this is one of them. Beginning and ending in writing anything is always a trouble of its own and it is a great trouble to any one doing any writing. That is where the newspaper is interesting, there is really of course no beginning and no ending to anything they are doing, it is when it is and in being when it is being there is no beginning and no ending.

That is because it exists any of every day and any of every day is not mixed up with beginning and ending.

That is a very interesting thing in writing in a newspaper in a newspaper being existing there is no beginning and no ending and in a way too there is no going on. One really has to think of everything as one thinks of anything and that is one thing.

I love my love with a b because she is peculiar. One can say this. That has nothing to do with what a newspaper does and that is the reason why that is the reason that newspapers and with it history as it mostly exists has nothing to do with anything that is living.

I said newspapers make things too easy and I said that once to a reporter and he said you have no idea I am sure how terribly hard we work. Yes I

37

said but after you have done all that hard work you have to write it up as it would be if you had known it all beforehand and that is what really makes it too easy. There is no discovery there is mostly no discovery in a newspaper or in history, they find out things they never knew before but there is no discovery and finally if all this goes on long enough it is all too easy.

I cannot come back too often to telling and hearing to talking and listening, to repeating and changing to knowing and remembering to having an intention of intending something or to have anything happening, all these things are as they are and one of them can never be another one of them no matter how commonly any one that is every one is in any confusion about them. I tell you and I cannot tell it to you too often although I may not tell it often enough as anybody even I can change about something I cannot tell it to you often enough that confusion is either making things easy by knowing beforehand how it is going to be done or by mixing up talking and listening, remembering and knowing not beginning and ending, and that is a very interesting thing think of that that there is really no confusion in mixing up beginning and ending no none at all.

And so now that we have gotten here that is now that we are not only writing the newspaper as well as reading what it writes what is it that it does do that makes it too easy to do and to read what it does do.

You see there is no beginning and ending because every day is the same that is that every day has anything that it has happening.

Now that is the difference between existing and happening.

If you exist any day you are not the same as any other day no nor any minute of the day because you have inside you being existing. Anybody who is existing and anybody really anybody is existing anybody really is that.

38

But anything happening well the inside and the outside are not the inside and the outside inside.

Let me do that again. The inside and the outside, the outside which is outside and the inside which is inside are not when they are inside and outside are not inside in short they are not existing, that is inside, and when the outside is entirely outside that is is not at all inside then it is not at all inside and so it is not existing. Do you not see what a newspaper is and perhaps history.

No matter how hard you work the result that you have is that the outside is outside and when it is outside it is not begun and when it is outside it is not ended and when it is neither begun nor ended it is not either a thing which has existed it is simply an event.

It is very curious in a newspaper that sometimes really sometimes a personality breaks through an event, it takes a tremendously strong personality to break through the events in a newspaper and when they do well it is soon over it is soon smoothed over and even history wishes to change it into something that any one could recover from.

In a novel in a play no matter what it is that happens it is hoped that nothing will be smoothed over that every minute of that novel there is a beginning and ending that always any personality that any one has there is one that no one can ever change into something that any one can recover from.

And the reason why is this. The more a novel is a novel the more a play is a play the more a writing is a writing the more no outside is outside outside is inside inside is inside.

I love my love with a b because she is peculiar.

39

There is something very odd that has happened in all this in connection with detective stories and now listen.

As I say beginning and ending has something to do with everything that is anything and so listen.

In real life that is if you like in the newspapers which are not real life but real life with the reality left out, the reality being the inside and the newspapers being the outside and never is the outside inside and never is the inside outside except in the rare and peculiar cases when the outside breaks through to be inside because the outside is so part of some inside that even a description of the outside cannot completely relieve the outside of the inside.

And so in the newspapers you like to know the answer in crime stories in reading crime and in written crime stories knowing the answer spoils it. After all in the written thing the answer is a let down from the interest and that is so every time that is what spoils most crime stories unless another mystery crops up during the crime and that mystery remains.

And then there is another very peculiar thing in the newspaper thing it is the crime in the story it is the detective that is the thing.

Now do you begin to see the difference between the inside and the outside.

In the newspaper thing it is the crime it is the criminal that is interesting, in the story it is the story about the crime that is interesting. Now think, you will perfectly realize that the newspaper practically never tells anything about detecting, a little in the case of Dillinger, a little in the case of Hauptmann but still really very little and in lesser crimes not at all the emphasis is entirely upon the crime and not upon the detecting and in the written story it is impossible to hold the attention by telling about the crime you can only hold the attention by telling about detecting. All this is very interesting

40

most most interesting and has to do with what the newspaper has to say and what it has not to say and the fact that in the long run one might say practically any day the newspaper is not really exciting.

I have said that the business of the artist is to be exciting and it is his business and if he is an artist whatever he does really does is really exciting. By exciting I mean it really does something to you really inside you.

Now is it the business of the newspapers is it the business of an historian to be exciting well I do not think so that is I do not think that it is the business of the newspaper to be exciting and I think in their hearts they really know this thing they know it is not their business to be exciting.

About the historian, the biographer and the autobiographer that is another matter and pretty soon later we will have to go into that.

What is it that is exciting, and how can exciting be soothing if it looks like excitement and is therefore soothing or if it is exciting and is therefore soothing or if it is as if it were exciting and is therefore soothing or not soothing, all these things have to be a great deal thought about if you are to understand anything if I am to understand anything about newspaper writing about any writing about anything being or not being written.

It is a very curious thing that a story told by any one about anything that has not really been exciting is exciting and a story told about anything that really has been exciting is not exciting.

It is a very curious thing this thing.

In thinking about plays I came to the conclusion that in real life the climax of a really exciting scene is completion and the climax of a made up exciting thing a written exciting thing is a relief and that it is not really possible to remember the climax of a real scene because you can not remember completion but you can remember relief.

Now the same thing is true when the newspaper tells about any real thing, the real thing having happened it is completed and being completed can not be remembered because the thing in its essence being completed there is no emotion in remembering it, it is a fact like any other and having been done it is for the purposes of memory a thing having no vitality. While anything which is a relief and in a made up situation as it gets more and more exciting when the exciting rises to being really exciting then it is a relief then it is a thing that has emotion when that thing is a remembered thing.

Now you must see how true this is about the crime story and the actual crime. The actual crime is a crime that is a fact and it having been done that in itself is a completion and so for purposes of memory with very rare exceptions where a personality connected with it is overpowering there is no memory to bother any one. Completion is completion, a thing done is a thing done and so it has in it no quality of ending or beginning. Therefore in real life it is the crime and as the newspaper has to feel about it as if it were in the act of seeing or doing it, they cannot really take on detecting they can only take on the crime, they cannot take on anything that takes on beginning and ending and in the detecting end of detective stories there is nothing but going on beginning and ending. Anybody does naturally feel that, that a detective is just that that detecting is just that that it is a continuity of beginning and ending and really nothing but that.

And so you have this curious situation. Newspapers are written as if what is happening is happening as they are writing and as it is happening in that way they can have in them no beginning and ending but after all they are writing and they are writing not as it is happening not as it the newspaper is printing or being read and yet all that has to be as if it were.

42

As I say they try to bridge the gap in every way. Head lines were invented to help them do this better, they are all taught exactly how it can be done and as they are so well taught finally it happens not as if it had begun but as if it had never been done. Finally the newspaper gets its readers so that it does not make any difference whether any event can or will happen as long as the newspaper can go on getting larger and larger with anything or smaller and smaller with anything, and always tell be telling that thing, that they are larger and larger and smaller and smaller in telling everything. That is what is finally happening that everybody has to know what everybody or anybody does but does anybody have it as a feeling what anybody or everybody does no not at all.

And so that is what the newspaper is.

And that brings us nearer and nearer to the writing of history of biography of autobiography, I keep getting nearer and nearer but am I really near enough.

We now know what the newspaper is and what it does and why it has to be made easier and easier because the more completely in every way everybody anybody knows anything knows everything that is always happening the more easily, the more easy it is to make it easy for any one to know this thing what is always happening.

A newspaper man is trained to make this easy by never changing, nothing must ever be changing, things are happening but nothing must ever be changing about their being happening, the newspaper must never give to any one reading it a feeling that anything is changing about something being always happening, if it ever could or would or should then any one would come to have some suspicion that there might be a beginning and ending to

43

anything and if there is a beginning and ending to anything then it destroys the simplicity of something always happening.

It is all a very curious thing but this is a true story of newspaper writing and the detective fiction just completely the other way progresses by a continuous beginning and ending and once more therefore destroys itself into not existing. It is too bad because it might have been yes it might have been something but always beginning and ending is as destructive to existing as never beginning and ending.

You do see this thing.

And now let us begin to think about another thing, about the feeling of a thing being existing even when it is a happening as the newspaper has it be.

Is a thing realler because not that you have really seen it but you have seen the place where it did happen. That is to say is there more beginning and end to it if you know what it looks like the place the actual place where the thing happened.

It seems to have more beginning and ending to it then and perhaps it really has not really has but gives the emotion of reality somewhat clearer.

It is for this reason that local newspapers have a different way of saying that anything is happening from metropolitan newspapers. The small local newspaper has the feeling that they are telling not what is happening as something that is happening but they are telling what happened to some one whom every one may or may not know but might know and certainly any one does know the exact spot the very place where the thing that happened has happened, that makes small town newspapers have a slightly different feeling about what is happening than the big newspaper and therefore they might if they were not a newspaper they might bring any one that is

44

every one to have the feeling that writing which is not what is happening gives any one.

Why is it that even the small newspaper which has to help them the local feeling of the place the actual place that anything that has happened why have they no intensity in their writing such as any one describing anything made up inside them can give to that writing.

Why is it.

Oh why is it.

Think of Defoe, he tried to write Robinson Crusoe as if it were exactly what did happen and yet after all he is Robinson Crusoe and Robinson Crusoe is Defoe and therefore after all it is not what is happening it is what is happening to him to Robinson Crusoe that makes what is exciting every one. You cannot go over it too often and so you can come you will come to know everything about anything being written.

I have come as far as this and it is really quite far to have come yes it is it really is quite far to have come and still all history and autobiography and biography have yet to come that is it is here but we have yet to come to know how and where it does come from.

Next time I am going to write more history for you, autobiography I have already done, biography I have already done I will tell you about that one, and so slowly yes slowly I will come to some knowing what it is that makes anything what it is what it was and what it has become.

But really and truly all about history and biography and autobiography will be both finished and begun oh yes it will yes it will it really will be both finished and begun in the next one.

LECTURE 4

AFTER all anybody is as their land and air is. Anybody is as the sky is low or high, the air heavy or clear, anybody is as there is wind or no wind there. It is that which makes them and the arts they make and the work they do and the way they eat and the way they drink and the way they learn and everything.

The thing that bothers me that always bothers me is why and how a writing that sounds just like a writing that is creating, is not creating, it is a bothersome thing that. I have just been reading two books that have concentration imagination and they tell what they have to tell and they are interesting and all the time you know they know that they will not be books that anybody could possibly think of reading five years hence and why. It is easy to ask and to answer somehow but to really know why, you know they know I know that this is true but to really know the real reason why to really know what is the difference between any book having interest reality imagination and concentration and will not last and one that will last is a most difficult thing to do. Of course it is easy enough to know it after it has lasted, anybody of course could do that but to know now why to really know why now, well it is not easy it really is not easy at all to know to really know anything about this thing. I always have thought I always have wondered I do still think and wonder about this thing. Is it that it has to be told somehow enough the thing to be told or is it the thing to be told itself. I am wondering.

One of you brought me poetry to read the other day and I said remember that if you have to use strained words to say what you have to say by strain existing in the words that you are using, what feels to you a rare emotion becomes common-place not ordinary that is alright but just common-place and a common-place thing does not contain feeling. That is what makes a common-place thing a common-place thing, that that it does not contain feeling.

Let me say that so that you that is I cannot may not be mistaken in saying this thing.

What makes a thing as it is coming out in being said or written what makes that thing a common-place thing, not what is that they felt before they said anything that is always supposing that they stopped long enough to feel anything. Has anything anything to do with stopping long enough to feel anything is it or is it not so.

Let me get solidly down really solidly to one of any two things and that one is the audience there may be there is there could be there will be there can be there shall be there has been there or again is not an audience to any- thing. Anything is not alike to any audience and yet it is. That is what any one is inclined to know that any audience is not alike or is and is mostly either one that is not alike or is.

That is something that is really not anything and I have found out that it is made up of anything and that anything is that one thing.

What is an audience and why is anybody that is everybody always men- tioning that thing. Anybody can mention an audience it is perfectly extraor- dinary how often I myself have had it mentioned that an audience is an audience and yet after all what do I who hear them tell it or they who tell it to me know about it. I have really found out quite a good deal about what an audience is by a simple series of adventures with it. I have been without it, and I have been with it, I have been myself be it to myself and I I have almost

47

been without being it to myself and then I came suddenly to find myself having had it without hearing that I was going to have had it that is not an outside audience but myself to it and then I found out something about Shakespeare's sonnets and really this has something to do with history although perhaps perhaps although even I do not believe it even if I do which I do.

Then listen while I tell it but this I know anybody will do because it is something to tell which is not the telling of it. But nevertheless this I will do.

Writing was writing if it was being written and in it even if I was talking I was not talking as I was writing, nor was I writing as I was talking, why should any one do that, but think use your common sense why should really why why should any one do that.

Just really why should any one do that that is why do I not do that of course I do not nobody should do that.

And this is the reason why.

As I say anybody is as their land and air and water sky and wind and anything else is and everything always is, it is not curiously not necessary to look out of the window to know that and yet everybody can need to do that they need to look out of the window not to find out what is what but for two reasons one reason is that they look out of the window which is what they do and the other is that as they look they look out of the window, not because of anything not because of that. Really and truly has any one more curiosity than they have and what can they do about it.

I saw a fire engine house to-day that was exactly like the ones they used to be when I was a child even inside to the man sitting and yawning while he was waiting, he was waiting for a fire and sometimes a fire comes. There

48

is no why not about that because sometimes a fire alarm comes and sometimes the fire comes and it was exactly as I remembered although if I had
to try to tell about it I would not have quite remembered not quite remembered particularly how the doors looked in proportion to the buildings.

But to come back to the audience because after all there is no one who can
be one if he is not one and so sometimes this can happen that no one alone
has been no one has been one audience to that thing. I was, to that fire
engine house. I really was I was just that thing I was one audience nothing
was happening that is to say the building was exciting but it always had
been, what would be the matter with it if it had not been. Very well then
an audience did I always have one have I always been one, am I one, when
anything is no longer happening, look alike if you like and then be that one
of any one or two of them.

So then the audience is the thing. It helps a lot to know anything about
this thing if you think are always really always thinking about the narrating
of anything of narrative being existing.

So then what did I know about myself as an audience.

I wondered often when I was quite young and watching and still I am
doing that thing watching anything inside me happen in relation to myself
or in relation to any one what any one being as it were as if they were to be
as I was where and when I am would believe as to what was happening. Do
you see what I mean. That is the beginning anyhow one beginning of an
audience being existing. And always anybody can know that always there is
no such thing existing as any one really not knowing as if it were anything of
any one else what is going on as if it were going on. When that happens they
call it introspection but call it what you like it is after all anybody or nobody

49

watching. I suppose inevitably if any one is going to be anybody telling anything and knowing anything of telling anything they are bound to begin with this thing, why not since after all you have to know less about it than about any other thing because nobody can do any contradicting because after all there it is and it is not at all there and it is not all there and nobody who says yes can say no and nobody who says yes can say no and nobody can say yes I know or no I know nobody no nobody at all because after all there is nothing there at all and that is something to which if there is there is no no no yes and there is no I guess. Nothing at all and all is such a comfort as it is where it is. That is what anybody who is to know how they are to tell what they are to tell is sure to have as all there is as well. And so they begin so. This you all of you know.

Then after all what is the use as you all all of you know this. So then beside as any one can come to be certain of then if it is as it is that is an audience is what it is what is it if an audience is this, pretty soon then can feel again that an audience is this, and then introspection can go on but the habit of this thing makes it cease to be this, because the audience and is it this keeps going on and so finally since it is all one, even when it is not this and it commences then not to go on being this although of course although of course yes it always will go on.

That is one, that is one audience then this.

So then we go on.

And then gradually anything goes on that is to say it is does not go on but any way there is anything there any way and is any one that is are you the audience for that too that is to say do you see it when it is there and is it there and what have you to say, what have you to say.

50

What is it to be an audience, I tell I must get down solidly to that what is it to be to have an audience what is it and is it the same thing or is it.

What is it.

That is to say can does any one separate themselves from the land so they can see it and if they see it are they the audience of it or to it. If you see anything are you its audience and if you tell anything are you its audience, and is there any audience for it but the audience that sees or hears it. And if you do do that to yourself or anything else you see does that after all begin what you began when you were it as it happened to come to be it or not. Who is alike when everybody looks at anybody and which is like which, the thing which has been seen or the thing which is prepared for it that is prepared to be seen because after all who cannot who will not prepare it. Really no one, when you come to think about it and yet every one does, does not prepare it. And all this has so much to do with writing a narrative of anything that I can almost cry about it.

I will try to be as simple as I can.

I had a funny experience once, this was a long time after I had been writing anything and everything as you all more or less have come to know it, it was about five years ago and I said I would translate the poems of a young french poet.

I did this not because of the poetry but because of the poet he had been very nice to me and I was grateful for it and so I wanted to make him happy and the way to show it was to translate the poetry of the young french poet.

So I began to translate and before I knew it a very strange thing had happened.

Hitherto I had always been writing, with a concentration of recognition

51

of the thing that was to be existing as my writing as it was being written. And now, the recognition was prepared beforehand there it was it was already recognition a thing I could recognize because it had been recognized before I began my writing, and a very queer thing was happening.

The words as they came out had a different relation than any words I had hitherto been writing, as they came out they had a certain smoothness they went one into the other in a different kind of fashion than any words ever had done before any words that I had ever written and I was perplexed at what was happening and I finished the whole thing not translating but carrying out an idea which was already existing and then suddenly I realized something I realized that words come out differently if there is no recognition as the words are forming because recognition had already taken place.

I concluded then that Shakespeare's sonnets were not written to express his own emotion I concluded that he put down what some one told him to do as their feeling which they definitely each time for each sonnet as their feeling and that is the reason that the words in the sonnets come out with a smooth feeling with no vibration in them such as the words in all his plays have as they come out from them.

Now anybody really ought to know this now really anybody should and anybody can know how this has to do with what every one always wants to know what has anybody's hearing anything have to do with their being an audience to anything, and what has being an audience or having an audience or having been an audience have to do with anything that is to say what has it all to do with telling anything.

Everybody always says do you write for an audience well do you and what is an audience and is it almost impossible or is it possible to make an audience of yourself and is it almost impossible or is it possible to rid yourself of yourself as an audience. And anyhow what has an audience to do with it. Well in a way everything and of course what they really mean by an audience when they say audience well perhaps really nothing nothing at all and yet perhaps everything.

As I say I have been very bothered about everything and I will tell about something else. When you are talking is it the same as when you are writing and when you are writing is it the same as when you are lecturing and when you are lecturing is it the same as knowing what history is and is knowing what history is is it the same as writing autobiography, and is it all alike because after all if you know what you are doing are you always doing it in the same way and then there is letter writing. I must only I have forgotten to do it write a whole long history of this thing that is what letter writing is because now I know.

There is one thing undoubted talking, writing and listening are not the same thing, and I will tell you why. When you talk you talk that is to say what you say has no importance mostly to any audience because any audience has no feeling that they are an audience not while everybody is just talking and this of course includes yourself and since any audience when you are just talking has no feeling that they are any audience then are they an audience and quite rightly you do not cannot must not shall not write as you talk, which of course you do not even when you say you do which anybody does say they do only of course not of course it is not true.

When you write this is of course recognition there is the recognition that you recognize what you write as you write, while as you talk there is of course some recognition but really is there any real recognition recognition of what

53

you talk as you talk. I myself think not, and therefore naturally not you do not write as you talk, because as you write you recognize what you write as you write and as you talk you do not recognize what you talk as you talk. There really is no real reason why you should since after all you are not your audience as you talk nobody really is not really as anybody talks that is just talks.

I knew I would have to do something else before I could begin to tell anything I know anything about history and now I know what it is I must know something about conversation and this is what I do know about conversation that is about talking.

You can see how difficult the writing of history is, I think anybody can see from this that is because conversation that is talking is what it is newspapers are what they are, mystery stories are what they are and anybody is what they are and anything that is anywhere where anybody is is what it is. You can see it is difficult very difficult that history can ever come to be literature. But it would be so very interesting if it could be so very interesting. Anybody can see that there is more confusion that is to say perhaps not more confusion but that it is a more difficult thing to write history to make it anything than to make anything that is anything be anything because in history you have everything, you have the newspapers and the conversations and letter writing and the mystery stories and audiences and in every direction an audience that fits anything in every other way in which any audience can fit itself to be anything, and there is of course as I have been saying so much to trouble any one about any one of any of these things.

And now before anything else to continue that is to begin that is to go on about letter writing. Letter writing is a very interesting part of audience

54

writing. When you are young you write about yourself inside or what you are doing or you write a letter of overwhelming that is a love letter or a mixture of this thing and in all this writing the audience is in a state of diffusion, and the letter is as it is as any of you may know, that is to say you write as if anybody was hearing only you have the vagueness of knowing that no one is hearing, the question of listening does not yet come in.

Adult letter writing is directed to some one even if the same thing is said as is said to any one any other one to whom you are then that is at that time writing but nevertheless it is directed to some one and the audience is not a diffused one but it is a distant one and how does that effect letter writing, well you know something about this thing and it really is the only time in writing when the outside and the inside flow together without interrupting, not generally with much concentrating, but still at any rate with not much interrupting. It is the one time when writing for an outside does not make the inside outside or the outside inside it is a diffusion but not a confusing, it is really a kind of an imitation of marrying of two being one, and yet being two and presumably two as much as anything. There can be a whole description of this thing but this is enough with which to begin.

And now before once more talking about something leading up to history let us finish with the subject of lecturing. Now in lecturing as in acting you introduce something else the physical the actual physical presence that connects the audience to the one doing anything and what does that do. Well anything does something that we are all beginning to know at the same time that we all know that anything does nothing.

One cannot of course go on forgetting that any one that is it is a natural thing that no one really not any one knows what any one means by what

55

they that is that one is saying and yet every one knowing this thing still always has to tell some one that is any one something. It is a well known fact that no human being can really stand not being able to tell some one something, you see an audience not understanding does not make any difference as long as any one can tell any one something. Any one travelling will tell any one even if that one does not understand the language the other one is talking will persistently attempt to tell that other one something.

So then although any one can say that they do not write for an audience and really why should they since anyway the audience will have its own feeling about anything nevertheless the writer writing knows what he is writing as he recognizes it as he is writing it and so he is actually having it happen that an audience is existing even if he as an audience is not an audience that is is one not having a feeling that he is an audience and yet that is just what a writer is. As he is a writer he is an audience because he does know what an audience is. He is not as one is when one is talking and every one is talking and talking is talking because then any one talking is not hearing what an audience is. What makes writing writing is hearing what an audience is that is to say makes recognition while in the act of writing what he is writing. It is so easy to know no not so easy to know and it is so easy to say no so hard to say but hard or easy it is said and known this what I have to say and do say as I say that is as I write.

Now in lecturing as I say another thing is happening there is the physical exciting, and that in a way destroys the physical something that a writer is while he is writing, because while he is writing that physical something by existing does not connect him with anything but concentrates him on recognition. That is the reason why the lecturer the debater the orator recognizes

56

what his audience hears but does not recognize what he himself says and that is very interesting. Of course if you are reading what you are lecturing then you have a half in one of any two directions, you have been recognizing what you are writing when you were writing and now in reading you disassociate recognizing what you are reading from what you did recognize as being written while you were writing. In short you are leading a double life. And that too may be interesting anything may be interesting but what has it to do with history writing, well something because a great many people about whom historians are writing have been orators or some such thing.

So then I do feel I am beginning to know a little more really a little more than I expected to be knowing about how history is and is to be and has been and might be written. After all can it be written.

It is certain that any man that is any human being at no time has the same feeling about anything as any one can have who tell them or to whom they tell anything, any one who is alone is alone but no one can have that thing happen and go on living that is continue to be alone and so any one that is every one is always telling any one anything or something.

That is what mysticism is, that is what the Trinity is, that is what marriage is, the absolute conviction that in spite of knowing anything about everything about how any one is never really feeling what any other one is really feeling that after all after all three are one and two are one. One is not one because one is always two that is one is always coming to a recognition of what the one who is one is writing that is telling. So there we have this which always has been and the historian along with all the things he has to tell has to tell this thing as if it were happening and it never is happening, the one is not one, the two are not one, the three are not one, and still in violent living, in

57

the thing that makes history what it is in the telling, the two although they are not one still again are not two and the three although they are not one are again not three.

We talked a great deal all this time we talked a great deal how hard it is to tell anything anything that has been anything that is, and that makes a narrative and that makes history and that makes literature and is history literature.

Well how far have we come.

Can history be literature when it has such a burden a burden of everything, a burden of so many days which are days one after the other and each day has its happening and still as in the newspaper what can make it matter if it is not happening to-day, the best thing that can happen about that happening is that it can happen again. And that makes the comfort of history to a historian that history repeats itself, that is really the only comfort that an historian can have from anything happening and really and truly it does not happen again not as it used to happen again because now we know really know so much that has happened that really we do know that what has happened does not happen again and so that for poor comfort has been taken away from the historian.

Of course if you like anything does happen again but when one does know as the historian now does know all the things that happened every day while it was happening then for the purpose of the historian history is no longer repeating and so the historian has now no comfort really none left to him.

And what is he to do, well that is a question, what is anybody to do about writing, well that is the question.

I personally think that the solution is that any one must amuse himself with anything and not think to recognize anything beside this thing, beside

58

playing with what he is playing with as he is writing what he is recognizing while the writing is being written by him.

What I mean is this, history has gotten to be so that anybody can if they go on know that everything that happened is what happened and as it all did happen it is a very serious thing that so much was happening. Very well then. What can be the addition to anything if everything is happening, look out of any window, any window nowadays is on a high building if it happens right and see what is happening. Well enough said, it is not necessary to go on with recognition, but soon you do know anybody can know, that it is all real enough. It all is all real enough, not only real enough but and that is where it is such a difficult thing not real enough for writing, real enough for seeing, almost real enough for remembering but remembering in itself is not really an important enough thing to really need recalling, insofar as it is not seeing, but remembering is seeing and so anything is an important enough thing for seeing but it is not an important enough thing for writing, it is an important enough thing for talking but not an important enough thing for telling.

That is really the trouble with what history is, it is important enough for seeing but not important enough for writing, it is important enough for talking but not important enough for telling. And that is what makes everybody so troubled about it all about what history is, because after all it ought to be important enough for telling for writing and not only important enough for talking and seeing, it really ought to be, it really ought to be, but can it be. Cannot it really be.

I feel about history the way I do about crime stories they ought to be they really ought to be they really ought to come to be literature but do they.

59

And so we always come back to what literature is.

What is literature.

Literature is the telling of anything but in telling that thing where is the audience. There is an audience of course there is an audience but where is that audience. Undoubtedly that audience has to be there for the purpose of recognition as the telling is proceeding to be written and that audience must be at one with the writing, must be at one with the recognition must have nothing of knowing anything before or after the recognition, and can that be true of the historian or of the newspaper man. No alas there have been some exceptions but are they really exceptions, not enough exceptions to really encourage any one.

The case of Boswell's Johnson is an interesting one, Boswell conceived himself as an audience an audience achieving recognition at one and the same time that Johnson achieved recognition of the thing he Johnson was saying, Johnson was saying those things as if he were writing those things that is achieving recognition of the thing while the thing was achieving expression and Boswell by the intensity of his merging himself in the immediacy of Johnson achieved recognition as Johnson himself was doing. But how can any historian do the same how can he, he would if he could but how can we, a newspaper man certainly cannot that I think I have certainly made plain as plain as it plainly cannot be done by the very thing the newspaper man has to really have to be done that is has to be done if the newspaper is to be what it is and of course the newspaper is to be what it is what it has had to become to have done what it has had to have done. But the historian well what can he do about it yes well what can he do about it. I wonder I do wonder what can he do about it.

The biographer has the same trouble, of course there is the other thing,

Vasari and Plutarch are like that, they make them up so completely that if they are not invented, they might as well be they do not really feel that any one of the ones about whom they tell had any life except the life they are given by their telling. That can happen and when it does it is writing, it is like historical plays and historical novels which can have that thing happen that really in writing the only existing the character has is the character the writer has given to them but how can an historian who knows everything really knows everything that has really been happening how can he come to have the feeling that the only existence the man he is describing has is the one he has been giving to him. How can he have this feeling, if he cannot then he cannot have the recognition while in the processes of writing, which writing really writing must really give to the one writing. After all the historian the historian who really knows everything and an historian really does he really does how can he have the creation of some one who has no existing except that the historian who is writing has at the moment of writing and therefore has as recognition at the moment of writing being writing. The historian is bound to have with him all the audience that has known every one about whom he is writing. It is worse than the wailing of the dead soldiers in L'Aiglon there are so many auditors there have been so many auditors, and there really can only be the one that is the one, and there are so many of them there have been so many of them and how can the historian lose them how can he how can he lose any of them and how can he lose all of them and if he does not how can history be writing that is be literature. How can it. Well I am sure I do not know.

It this thing, this thing that dimly worries any one who thinks about an historical anything which has induced every one, Mark Twain in A Yankee At King Arthur's Court and then all that have been written since then has made them attempt to in one way and another way try to make a thing a thing that they recognize while they are writing make it something that had no existing before that writing gave it that recognition, they tried to do this by changing something. Of course it is something to do but is it really interesting not interesting enough.

What can the historian do, well I do hope he will do something, I almost would like to be an historian myself to perhaps do something. You see that is why making it the Autobiography of Alice B. Toklas made it do something, it made it be a recognition by never before that writing having it be existing. It is a natural thing to do if writing is to be writing, but after all it ought to be able to be done as history as a mystery story. I am certain so certain so more than certain that it ought to be able to be done. I know so well all the causes why it cannot be done and yet if it cannot be done cannot it be done it would be so very much more interesting than anything if it could be done even if it cannot be done.

I wish it could be done and if it could be done all these reasons for its not having been done would be of no importance because it will have been done.

That is what makes anything everything that it has been done and so perhaps history will not repeat itself and it will come to be done. Perhaps no perhaps yes anyway this is all I know just at present about how writing is written how an audience is existing how any one telling anything is telling that thing.